Summary of

Eat Fat, Get Thin

by Mark Hyman, MD

Instaread

Please Note

This is a summary with analysis.

Copyright © 2016 by Instaread. All rights reserved worldwide. No part of this publication may be reproduced or transmitted in any form without the prior written consent of the publisher.

Limit of Liability/Disclaimer of Warranty: The publisher and author make no representations or warranties with respect to the accuracy or completeness of these contents and disclaim all warranties such as warranties of fitness for a particular purpose. The author or publisher is not liable for any damages whatsoever. The fact that an individual or organization is referred to in this document as a citation or source of information does not imply that the author or publisher endorses the information that the individual or organization provided. This concise summary is unofficial and is not authorized, approved, licensed, or endorsed by the original book's author or publisher.

Table of Contents

Overview 4

Important People 6

Key Takeaways 7

Analysis 10

Key Takeaway 1 10

Key Takeaway 2 12

Key Takeaway 3 14

Key Takeaway 4 16

Key Takeaway 5 17

Key Takeaway 6 19

Key Takeaway 7 21

Key Takeaway 8 23

Author's Style 25

Author's Perspective 26

References 28

Overview

Eat Fat, Get Thin is a science-driven nutrition and diet book that addresses dietary fat and how it impacts the body. By debunking long-held beliefs about fat, the book explains why fats are a crucial part of weight loss and any healthy diet. It offers readers a roadmap to incorporate more healthy fats into their daily routines.

Over the past century, a number of scientists have promoted research that supposedly proved that the fat people consume is the fat that ends up on their bodies. The US government, national health organizations, and the food industry picked up on these assumptions, and an anti-fat movement was born. This gave rise to an entire industry of low-fat "diet" foods. In the meantime, however, citizens of the United States grew more obese and developed more chronic diseases, particularly heart disease and diabetes. As it turned out, fats are not only essential to the way the human body functions, but they actually contribute to optimum health.

Olive oil, avocados, red meat, and coconut oil are among the many sources of healthy fats, and among those foods that have long been wrongly demonized. After adding these foods back into their diet, men and women can enjoy not only weight loss but many health benefits, such as cancer prevention and healthier skin. By following the 21-day Eat Fat, Get Thin Plan, dieters will quickly reap the benefits of their new high-fat, low-carb lifestyle.

Important People

Mark Hyman is a family physician, health and nutrition leader and advocate, and the author of *Eat Fat, Get Thin*. His own beliefs about dietary fat have changed over time as he observed results in his patients and in himself. He wrote this book to change the public perception of fat, a long-defamed nutrient.

Key Takeaways

1. The demonization of fat over the past several decades has had a significant impact, particularly in the United States, where obesity and chronic disease have become increasingly common.

2. The fat a person eats is not the fat that ends up on his or her body. Carbohydrates and sugar, not fat, are the culprits in weight gain and the onset of many chronic diseases.

3. The way the body gains and loses weight is not a simple math function of calories consumed and calories expended. The source of the calories matters more than the number.

4. Fat does not cause heart disease. In some cases, consuming fats can actually reverse or prevent certain ailments, including heart disease and diabetes.

5. The food industry has played a critical role in the demonization of fat.

6. Food is not just a source of energy. Food provides information to the body to help in a wide range of critical functions.

7. Both food and body are complex systems of interconnecting parts that interact with each

other, a perspective taken by practitioners of functional medicine.

8. The Eat Fat, Get Thin Plan has three steps: the planning phase, 21 weeks of strict dieting, and then the transition period into a long-term healthy lifestyle.

Thank you for purchasing this Instaread book

Download the Instaread mobile app to get unlimited text & audio summaries of bestselling books.

Visit Instaread.co to learn more.

Analysis

Key Takeaway 1

The demonization of fat over the past several decades has had a significant impact, particularly in the United States, where obesity and chronic disease have become increasingly common.

Analysis

Based on flawed scientific research, incorrect assumptions about fat and its role in health and disease have proliferated throughout the world, especially in the United States. Removing fat from the diet has actually given rise to more widespread obesity and chronic diseases. However, since misinformed assumptions about fat are so pervasive and treated as unquestioned fact, it's difficult to convince people to stop eating so many carbohydrates and sugars and to work fat back into their diets.

According to data from the National Center for Health Statistics (NCHS), 1977 was not only the year the low-fat diet was first recommended to US citizens. It was the same year that the rise in obesity rates first began to accelerate. Graphical representation of NCHS data shows a distinct correlation. It does not necessarily represent causation, but other scientific research has proven that low-fat diets have contributed to diseases such as obesity and diabetes. [1]

The numbers on obesity rates in the United States vary somewhat. According to Gallup, 28 percent of adults in the United States were obese as of 2015, a new record high. [2] The *Journal of the American Medical Association* reported a higher number for 2011-2012, citing a 34.9 percent obesity rate among US adults. [3] Obesity rates for that time period were highest among certain age groups and races, including non-Hispanic blacks at 47.8 percent, Hispanics at 42.5 percent, and middle-aged adults, 40 to 59 years old, at 39.5 percent. [4] However, according to Gallup, the rate of obesity in the white population has increased much faster than among blacks, Asians, and Hispanics, at more than double the rate of the other groups from 2008 to 2015. While the numbers may vary to an extent, in all cases, they are problematic. They are often the result of poor or simply misinformed diet choices, such as choosing a low-fat diet because the US government's official dietary guidelines concluded that fat was unhealthy.

Key Takeaway 2

The fat a person eats is not the fat that ends up on his or her body. Carbohydrates and sugar, not fat, are the culprits in weight gain and the onset of many chronic diseases.

Analysis

For decades, the US government, national health organizations, health researchers, and the food industry have professed that the fat a person eats is the fat that ends up around his or her hips, thighs, and midsection. However, this is not exactly true. The saturated fat that appears in the bloodstream and that has been linked to heart disease does not come from foods such as meat and nuts. The liver produces those particular saturated fats itself through lipogenesis following consumption of carbohydrates or alcohol, a form of sugar. As for body fat, carbohydrates, and not dietary fats, are what spikes insulin, which turns on the metabolic switch that leads to fat storage.

The debate surrounding reasons for weight gain has polarized scientists, health experts, and physicians. This has compelled non-experts to conduct their own investigations. One study, conducted for British science television, was self-administered by a set of twins, who were non-specialists. [5] One twin went on a no-carb diet, and one on a low-fat diet. The population of this study was intriguing because rarely do two people in dietary studies have the same DNA. Such a study can show how two different theories would work on two very similar genomes, which removes some of the genetic differences found in more diverse study population sets. However, this study's no-carb diet cut out fruits and vegetables, which are an essential part of the Eat Fat, Get Thin Plan.

In this study, both twins lost weight. The twin on the no-carb diet lost more weight than the twin on the low-fat diet, but the no-carb twin reported feeling sluggish and foggy. Being able to eat fruits and vegetables may have significantly changed the subject's negative responses to the no-carb diet, which included fatigue, constipation, and bad breath. The twins' conclusion was that trouble happens when mixing fat with carbs and sugars, such as saturated fat with carbs. This mix is common in processed foods, so cutting those out of a diet is a healthy choice.

Key Takeaway 3

The way the body gains and loses weight is not a simple math function of calories consumed and calories expended. The source of the calories matters more than the number.

Analysis

Many people believe the body governs weight gain and loss through a basic mathematical equation surrounding calories in, calories out, known as the energy balance hypothesis. Per that hypothesis, it does not matter whether an individual subsists on 1,800 daily calories of cookies and potato chips or 1,800 daily calories of fresh meats and produce; his or her weight would end up the same. However, studies show this simply isn't the case. Different calories impact the body and its processes in a variety of ways, including gene expression, hormonal balance, brain chemistry, immune system function, and gut bacteria. It's about the quality of calories, not quantity.

This understanding of weight gain and weight loss as calorie counting and energy balance is also problematic for people who are obese. It suggests they are incapable or unwilling to heal themselves, regardless of whether their overeating is genetic, environmental, or behavioral. [6] The other major problem with calorie counting for dieters is that calorie-restrictive diets are often unsustainable over the long term due to increased cravings and hunger pangs. Traditional dieting often doesn't work for this very reason because dieters yo-yo back and forth every time their calorie-deprived bodies can't resist cravings, particularly for carbs and sugars.

Key Takeaway 4

Fat does not cause heart disease. In some cases, consuming fats can actually reverse or prevent certain ailments, including heart disease and diabetes.

Analysis

Carbohydrates and sugar, not dietary fats, are the reason the liver produces more saturated fat in the bloodstream, which leads to clogged arteries and cardiovascular complications. Dietary fats have other functions for cholesterol, included raising levels of high-density lipoprotein (HDL), the "good" cholesterol, and the good type of low-density lipoprotein (LDL). Dietary fat reduces inflammation and risk for clotting, among other risk factors for developing heart disease. It also improves blood vessel health. The only problematic types of dietary fat for heart disease are trans fats and certain vegetable oils, such as soy, corn, and sunflower, though many experts still believe they are healthy.

A January 2016 study published in the *Journal of the American Heart Association* supports this theory. Although results varied from country to country, healthy fat intake was shown to be a factor in reducing risk for heart disease. [7] In some countries, people could lower their risk for heart disease by eating less trans fats, while in others, they could reduce their risk by boosting their intake of healthy polyunsaturated fats. Finding the optimum balance of the right fats, and not cutting out fat altogether, plays a role in alleviating the burden of heart disease and even extending life.

Key Takeaway 5

The food industry has played a critical role in the demonization of fat.

Analysis

As more scientists, doctors, and even the government began defaming dietary fat, food and beverage companies saw an opportunity to create an entire "diet" foods industry surrounding "low-fat" and "fat-free" foods. However, those products contained higher amounts of carbohydrates, sugars, and other unhealthy ingredients. Without realizing the health risks involved, consumers latched onto the diet foods industry that food companies had created.

Food companies have been frequent sources of funding for health associations and researchers who perform the studies that back the supposed safety and health benefits of a low-fat diet. Soft drink companies have been frequent targets of public health advocates for marketing products as "diet" that may not actually be healthy. These companies are criticized for their funding of research that argues that soda and diet soda can be part of a healthy diet. Coca-Cola Company was recently involved in a scandal for funding a nonprofit obesity research group. [8] The nonprofit funded by Coke had later concluded that exercise was more important to fighting obesity than diet. Health researchers balked at this claim, and the nonprofit eventually disbanded. The university affiliated with the organization returned a $1 million grant to Coca-Cola.

In the midst of this ordeal, Coca-Cola, in a move to demonstrate transparency, revealed that the company had contributed nearly $119 million in funding to scientific research and health and fitness programs since 2010. [9] Six months later, the company said it actually spent more during that time frame and updated the total to $132 million. This entire debacle illustrates the risks and potential biases involved when food and beverage companies fund scientific, health-based nutrition research. Regardless of whether industry-funded studies are biased in the food industry's favor, health experts and consumers tend to distrust study results that derive from corporate funding

Key Takeaway 6

Food is not just a source of energy. Food provides information to the body to help in a wide range of critical functions.

Analysis

Food is so much more than a way for the body to create energy, as the nutrients contained within can impact every biological process of the body. Food triggers genes on and off, which can mean triggering beneficial genes or genes that cause harm, depending on the food and nutrients it contains. Food can impact mood, focus, memory, and other critical brain functions. Food can create a balance or imbalance of the good and bad bacteria in the gut, which houses most of the immune system. The rising field of nutrigenomics is taking a closer look at the concept of food as biological information and coding for the body.

Many people treat food as nothing more than fuel to get them from one hunger pang to the next rather than as a code to tell their bodies how to operate. People might forget about a bite of food as soon as they take the next, but each bite of food is vital to the body and so should be treated with more forethought, if not reverence. Instead, many adults stuff bags of potato chips or packages of cookies into their mouths while their minds are focused on the television after a long day at work. Teenagers stay up late playing video games while drinking cans of soda and energy drinks. In these scenarios and with these habits, automated eating and drinking overpowers conscious thought about how food or drink choices help or hurt the body.

The ease and convenience of processed foods weakens the need for American consumers to make detailed decisions about food choices, which have become more flippant and inconsequential as easy access to fast food and processed foods has increased. For obesity rates to change, people need to give more consideration to food again and take pride in what they eat and, more importantly, what nutrients they put into their bodies.

Key Takeaway 7

Both food and body are complex systems of interconnecting parts that interact with each other, a perspective taken by practitioners of functional medicine.

Analysis

Scientific researchers have often tried to isolate certain foods, ingredients, body parts, or bodily processes to demonstrate dietary cause and effect, which has yielded questionable findings. Isolating nutrients or bodily processes and then trying to prove causality of one impacting the other is problematic because nutrients don't enter the body alone and thus don't act alone. They impact more than one bodily process and system at any given time. It's crucial to examine the body as a system where an imbalance in one area can contribute to disorders elsewhere, such as the relationship between weight management and metabolism. Systems biology and functional medicine take this perspective, and it has been essential for disproving false assertions and dietary recommendations about fat.

Nutrition and digestion are so complex that even individual parts can be broken down into their own systems of parts. For example, appetite is just one aspect of digestion, and the appetite control system has several parts, including aspects of the nervous system, digestive system, and immune system. [10] Appetite may seem as simple as someone feeling hungry, meaning that it must have been a while since the individual's last meal. But various factors can increase or decrease appetite, including the types of foods the individual last ate, physical activity, sleep, stress, mood, smells in the air, and even the thought of food. These factors impact the four parts of the appetite control system in various ways, which then determine whether the individual feels hungry. Appetite is just one aspect of nutrition and digestion that plays a vital role in weight loss, which demonstrates the complexity of controlling and achieving weight loss.

Key Takeaway 8

The Eat Fat, Get Thin Plan has three steps: the planning phase, 21 weeks of strict dieting, and then the transition period into a long-term healthy lifestyle.

Analysis

The first step of the plan requires two days of preparation. Physical preparation involves ridding the kitchen of all unhealthy foods. Mental preparation involves removing all food-related temptations, such as a late-night pizza delivery menu, and resolving any lingering concerns about the healthfulness of fat. For the next 21 weeks, following the diet plan is priority, but important support systems include exercise, proper sleep, and relaxation. In the final phase, the individual can stay on the same dietary program or transition to a long-term Pegan diet. The Pegan diet takes the best of the Paleo and vegan diets to create something healthy but sustainable over the long term.

For decades, studies have shown that removing temptation is more powerful than willpower alone. Modern willpower studies date back to the "marshmallow test" of the late 1960s and early 1970s. [11] The study tested children's ability to delay gratification by resisting eating the marshmallow in front of them for the reward of two marshmallows later. A more recent study, published in *Neuron* in 2013, confirmed the benefits of removing temptation over depending on sheer willpower. [12] These findings certainly apply to unhealthy foods and beverages, which are a common personal reward in times of both celebration and stress. Therefore, when people remove unhealthy products from their kitchen, they are doing their future selves a favor by not wearing down their willpower.

Author's Style

As a physician, Mark Hyman makes science the centerpiece of his arguments by frequently citing studies to demonstrate why people profess certain things about fats and nutrition. In Chapter 2, for example, he formulates a long timeline of studies to show the progression of research and how fat became demonized over time. Hyman also describes how these studies were conducted and includes other important details that could impact analysis of the results. He frequently breaks down these studies and describes how they may not accurately portray their findings. This could be due to unreliable data sourcing, short timeline, small population of study participants, or general cherry-picking or skewing of the results. He even makes suggestions for the types of studies he would like to see done, which would better demonstrate whether long-held assumptions about fat and health are actually true.

Hyman explains the biological and nutrigenomic aspects of fat and how it affects the human body. However, he spends much of the book debunking what he refers to as "myths" propagated for decades by misguided scientists, the food industry, and the government. Hyman mentions that many of his patients have benefited from the Eat Fat, Get Thin Plan, and he includes the occasional story or testimonial to that effect. However, he mainly focuses on the science that backs his dietary recommendations.

Author's Perspective

Mark Hyman is a family physician who has offered his theories about a fatty diet to his own patients. Their successes, and the success he had with the diet himself, convinced Hyman to change the way he thought about dietary fats and their effects on the body. Hyman understands the body and food as a series of complex, intertwining systems. He publicly shares this belief through his work as Pritzker Foundation Chair in Functional Medicine at Cleveland Clinic and as the director of the Cleveland Clinic for Functional Medicine. He is a nine-time No. 1 *New York Times* bestselling author and world-renowned speaker, educator, and advocate in the realms of health and nutrition.

~~~~ END OF INSTAREAD ~~~~

Thank you for purchasing this Instaread book

Download the Instaread mobile app to get unlimited text & audio summaries of bestselling books.

Visit Instaread.co to learn more.

References

1. "Health, United States, 2008: With Special Feature on the Health of Young Adults." National Center for Health Statistics. March 2009. Accessed April 8, 2016. http://www.ncbi.nlm.nih.gov/books/NBK19623/figure/chartbook.f7/?report=objectonly

2. Witters, Dan. "U.S. Obesity Rate Climbs to Record High in 2015." Gallup. February 12, 2016. Accessed March 26, 2016. http://www.gallup.com/poll/189182/obesity-rate-climbs-record-high-2015.aspx

3. Ogden, Cynthia L., et al. "Prevalence of Childhood and Adult Obesity in the United States, 2011-2012." *Journal of the American Medical Association* 311:8 (2014): 806-814. Accessed April 11, 2016. http://jama.jamanetwork.com/article.aspx?articleid=1832542

4. Centers for Disease Control and Prevention. "Adult Obesity Facts." Accessed March 26, 2016. http://www.cdc.gov/obesity/data/adult.html

5. Van Tulleken, Alexander. "One twin gave up sugar, the other gave up fat. Their experiment could change your life." *Daily Mail.* January 27, 2014. Accessed March 25, 2016. http://www.dailymail.co.uk/health/article-2546975/One-twin-gave-sugar-gave-fat-Their-experiment-change-YOUR-life.html

6. Taubes, Gary. "What Makes You Fat: Too Many Calories, or the Wrong Carbohydrates?" *Scientific American.* September 1, 2013. Accessed March 25, 2016. http://www.scientificamerican.com/article/what-makes-you-fat-too-many-calories-or-the-wrong-carbohydrates/

7. Wang, Qianyi, et al. "Impact of Nonoptimal Intakes of Saturated, Polyunsaturated, and Trans Fat on Global Burdens of Coronary Heart Disease." *Journal of the American Heart Association.* November 18, 2015. Accessed April 8, 2016. http://jaha.ahajournals.org/content/5/1/e002891.full

8. O'Connor, Anahad. "Research Group Funded by Coca-Cola to Disband." *The New York Times.* December 1, 2015. Accessed March 26, 2016. http://well.blogs.nytimes.com/2015/12/01/research-group-funded-by-coca-cola-to-disband/

9. Associated Press. "Coca-Cola says it spent more on health research and partnerships than it previously disclosed." *U.S. News & World Report.* March 24, 2016. Accessed March 26, 2016. http://www.usnews.com/news/business/articles/2016-03-24/coke-discloses-more-of-its-funding-on-health-efforts

10. Hyman, Mark. "Systems Biology: The Gut-Brain—Fat Cell Connection and Obesity." *Alternative Therapies.* January/February 2006.

Accessed March 26, 2016. http://drhyman.com/downloads/Biology-of-Obesity.pdf

11. Mischel, Walter, et al. "Delay of gratification in children." *Science*. May 26, 1989. Accessed April 8, 2016. http://science.sciencemag.org/content/244/4907/933

12. Crockett, Molly, et al. "Restricting Temptations: Neural Mechanisms of Precommitment." *Neuron*. July 24, 2013. Accessed April 8, 2016. http://www.cell.com/neuron/abstract/S0896-6273(13)00448-0

CPSIA information can be obtained
at www.ICGtesting.com
Printed in the USA
LVOW04s0803140516
488253LV00029B/480/P

Summary of

The Phoenix Project

by Gene Kim, Kevin Behr, and George Spafford

Instaread

Please Note

This is a summary with analysis.

Copyright © 2016 by Instaread. All rights reserved worldwide. No part of this publication may be reproduced or transmitted in any form without the prior written consent of the publisher.

Limit of Liability/Disclaimer of Warranty: The publisher and author make no representations or warranties with respect to the accuracy or completeness of these contents and disclaim all warranties such as warranties of fitness for a particular purpose. The author or publisher is not liable for any damages whatsoever. The fact that an individual or organization is referred to in this document as a citation or source of information does not imply that the author or publisher endorses the information that the individual or organization provided. This concise summary is unofficial and is not authorized, approved, licensed, or endorsed by the original book's author or publisher.

Table of Contents

Overview 5

Important People 7

Key Takeaways 9

Analysis 12

Key Takeaway 1 12

Key Takeaway 2 14

Key Takeaway 3 15

Key Takeaway 4 17

Key Takeaway 5 18

Key Takeaway 6 20

Key Takeaway 7 21

Key Takeaway 8 22

Key Takeaway 9 23

Key Takeaway 10 24

Key Takeaway 11 25

Instaread on The Phoenix Project

Key Takeaway 12 26

Author's Style 27

Author's Perspective 29

References 31

Overview

When the Phoenix launch fails, the company's chief executive officer gives the IT department an ultimatum to meet its obligations or be outsourced. Another crisis arises, and Palmer resigns because the CEO undermines his strategy. Days later, the CEO invites Palmer to rejoin the company with his apologies because the board members, and Reid especially, showed him that his actions prevented the IT department from functioning. Reid supervises the IT department as it ceases to take on new work, then slowly resumes normal obligations, all the while creating a structure based on DevOps principles.

As the IT department begins working more cohesively, it develops new projects to push recommendations and customized discounts to customers and automate the process of setting up testing environments. The department engages in constant improvement and preventive projects, closes monitoring gaps, and randomly tests emergency and security response. Once all of these changes are made and the IT department is operating in accordance with the Three Ways of DevOps and monitoring the four types of work, the company's market share rises and it is profitable enough that the board decides not to split up the company or outsource IT. The CEO offers to put Palmer on a track to become the chief operating officer in two years.

Important People

Gene Kim is the co-founder of open source security and compliance automation company Tripwire and author of several books about DevOps and Visible Ops.

Kevin Behr founded the Information Technology Process Institute and is the chief information officer's chief strategist at the consultancy he founded, Assemblage Pointe.

George Spafford is a research director for Gartner on the subject of DevOps and other IT strategies.

Eliyahu Goldratt (1947-2011) wrote the classic management novel *The Goal: A Process of Ongoing Improvement* (1984), on which *The Phoenix Project* is patterned.

Bill Palmer is the fictional vice president of IT for Parts Unlimited and the narrator for *The Phoenix Project*.

Steve Masters is the CEO of Parts Unlimited.

Wes Davis is the director of Distributed Technology Operations at Parts Unlimited.

Patty McKee is the director of IT Service Support at Parts Unlimited.

Sarah Moulton is the senior vice president of Retail Operations at Parts Unlimited.

Erik Reid is a potential board member and former factory director at Parts Unlimited.

Brent Geller is a lead engineer in the IT department at Parts Unlimited.

John Pesche is the chief information security officer (CISO) at Parts Unlimited.

Key Takeaways

1. Business failings that prevent IT productivity generally involve disregarding the importance of IT and not providing IT with the autonomy and resources it needs.

2. Development and operations work better when they are considered two halves of the same team, not competitors. Their cooperation is necessary to improve the complete resource chain for the many steps between a business goal and deployment.

3. Making work in process visible requires complete awareness of resource spending and control over which projects are released from the queue. Releasing work should be decided based on availability of the most limiting resource, also called the constraint.

4. Once the constraint of a process is identified, the next responsibilities of the team are to exploit the constraint and to subordinate the constraint by making it less necessary. Improvement to the deployment pipeline anywhere but at the point of constraint results in no gains.

5. The ultimate goal of documenting the deployment pipeline is to ensure that a process can be replicated and eventually automated, if possible.

6. The more utilized a particular resource is, the longer tasks will wait in a queue before receiving

hands-on attention. These wait times multiply when a task is handed off between work stations multiple times.

7. If a team is not constantly improving itself in some way, entropy guarantees that its skills are decreasing.

8. The four types of work are business tasks, internal IT projects, changes, and unplanned recovery work that travels backward through the deployment pipeline.

9. The First Way of DevOps states that all work must flow from development to IT to the customer. This flow should be maximized and free of defects.

10. The Second Way of DevOps states that feedback should flow from the customer to IT, and from IT to development. It must be amplified to prevent problems, improve detection and recovery, and improve overall quality.

11. The Third Way of DevOps states that a business's IT culture should support experimentation, risk-taking, and the learning and practice that facilitate mastery.

12. DevOps strategies apply to departments that already use other structures, use open source or proprietary software, or are of any size or flexibility.

Thank you for purchasing this Instaread book

Download the Instaread mobile app to get unlimited text & audio summaries of bestselling books.

Visit Instaread.co to learn more.

Analysis

Key Takeaway 1

Business failings that prevent IT productivity generally involve disregarding the importance of IT and not providing IT with the autonomy and resources it needs.

Analysis

Prior to the restructuring of the IT department at Parts Unlimited, the project manager had no idea how many projects the employees were working on in a given day. Work in process was completely invisible, so resources were constantly stressed as they were given more tasks than the department could handle. The lack of oversight caused a high level of accidents, which resulted in unplanned work.

In many other professions, the lack of awareness of a department's obligations would be considered a crime or a hazard to life and limb. In a police department, if the police officers and detectives did not keep track of their work in process and inform supervisors of their tasks, a suspect's rights could be violated, a victim's report might never be investigated, and emergency calls might go unanswered. In a hospital, invisible work in process could lead to patients ignored in their beds and tests left incomplete. In those cases, failure to monitor and follow up on work in progress would result in work being redone. Hospitals that draw blood and fail to test it or store it properly would need to draw another sample.

Key Takeaway 2

Development and operations work better when they are considered two halves of the same team, not competitors. Their cooperation is necessary to improve the complete resource chain for the many steps between a business goal and deployment.

Analysis

At Parts Unlimited, the company's IT super-tribe included the vice president, the CEO, the CISO, the directors of smaller departments, the engineers, the developers, and anyone else whose work contributed to the deployment pipeline. Separation of responsibilities and resources prevented them from understanding what they needed to provide to each other in order to achieve the final goal.

Isolation between teams in a single organization is sometimes called siloing, and it presents a challenge to all companies that divide teams and force them to compete for budget, fight for vital resources, such as IT support, and push blame for an error out of the department to prevent budget penalties. Manhattan's chief US prosecutor said in September 2015 that one reason automaker General Motors failed to report safety issues or issue a recall for a dangerous ignition switch was because reporting responsibilities were spread across departments, which did not communicate about what they knew, so that no one had the complete picture that would have triggered the recall. [1] In IT, siloing can cause enormous security gaps if one department assumes that customer data safety is another department's responsibility.

Key Takeaway 3

Making work in process visible requires complete awareness of resource spending and control over which projects are released from the queue. Releasing work should be decided based on availability of the most limiting resource, also called the constraint.

Analysis

The IT department at Parts Unlimited started out with no way to control what work was in process and how tasks were released to the team. After witnessing the way that a manufacturing plant controlled task release, however, Palmer established new procedures for understanding which projects the various departments were working on, what resources were strained, and how to best utilize their constraint, a lead engineer named Brent.

A simple way of thinking about a constraint is with the chemistry concept of the limiting reagent. Every process requires a set amount of its inputs, which can be materials, workers, or time, in order to create a quantum of output. In a non-technical example, if a recipe for cookies requires two cups of flour and a bag of chocolate chips, among other ingredients, and the baker has four cups of flour and one bag of chips, he or she can still only make one batch of cookies even though there is enough flour to make two batches. The amount of chocolate chips limits the number of batches to one, and it would be a bad idea to start the second batch of cookies before the baker has purchased more chocolate chips. In the IT department, the limiting reagent was Brent's available time, and sending something through the deployment pipeline before Brent had more time would only result in the project simply spending time in a queue.

Key Takeaway 4

Once the constraint of a process is identified, the next responsibilities of the team are to exploit the constraint and to subordinate the constraint by making it less necessary. Improvement to the deployment pipeline anywhere but at the point of constraint results in no gains.

Analysis

Since Brent was the constraint at Parts Unlimited's IT department, Palmer found ways to protect Brent's working time to ensure he spent it only on the most important tasks. Improving the system at the constraint improved the efficiency of the entire pipeline.

An analogy for understanding this process is finding the most effective way to filter water. The flow of water from its dirty state to being cleaned of impurities represents the production pipeline, and the filter itself is the constraint. Dumping water into the filter faster will not result in more water coming out of the filter. However, once the filter has been identified as a constraining factor, the process of pouring the water can be sped up by ensuring that the filter is not used for anything else that might clog it, like oil, and that it always has a consistent volume of water flowing through it. Subordinating the constraint of the filter would involve setting up another filter to double output or using lower-grade filters on less important filtering tasks.

Key Takeaway 5

The ultimate goal of documenting the deployment pipeline is to ensure that a process can be replicated and eventually automated, if possible.

Analysis

Documentation at the Parts Unlimited IT department involved recording the step-by-step processes for tasks that were done often or which could have had repercussions on other parts of the business. The department documented changes to ensure that the changes did not conflict with each other and to be able to trace the possible causes of service outages. They also documented Brent's activities so that other people could do the same tasks later on, freeing up Brent's time, and so that some of those tasks could eventually be automated to further remove the potential for mistakes.

Some of the popular discourse around the automation of labor focuses on its ability to replace humans and force them out of jobs, but in an environment like the Parts Unlimited IT department, automation did not create the opportunity for employees to be laid off. [2] Instead, automation permitted the same number of employees to do more. Completing all of the tasks that were automated by instead hiring more people would have cost the business an excessive amount of money and could still have resulted in redundant work, or work being redone, as those new people learned their jobs and made human mistakes. Identifying work that could not be automated, but which could be done by people other than Brent, freed Brent up to do work only he could do using his knowledge of the company's systems, ensuring that he still had a job even while his tasks were taken away and given to other employees.

Key Takeaway 6

The more utilized a particular resource is, the longer tasks will wait in a queue before receiving hands-on attention. These wait times multiply when a task is handed off between work stations multiple times.

Analysis

Palmer and his teammates discovered that a relatively quick task that required Brent's work would actually take more than 63 hours because it would be handed off between seven work stations that were each 90 percent utilized. That waiting time needed to be considered in timelines for projects.

The determination of how much time a project waits in a queue at a work station depends on what the unit of time is in that particular workplace. In lean manufacturing, time is measured in cycles, which is the amount of time it takes to complete a particular task from the start of one iteration to the start of the next. [3] For example, if an IT department often must revoke privileges to a particular user account, the cycle time could be the amount of time it takes to log in, navigate to the network access policies, make a change, save it, and close out that process by logging out. Depending on the type of network, this could take a few minutes or an hour.

Key Takeaway 7

If a team is not constantly improving itself in some way, entropy guarantees that its skills are decreasing.

Analysis

The Improvement Kata that is part of Toyota's manufacturing strategy encourages employees to engage in a routine of improvement. They may improve anything, as long as they are not remaining stagnant, because a team is never truly in a static state. If things are not improving, something is in decline.

It might be helpful to think of IT capabilities like a muscle. For example, once a weightlifter has developed the ability to lift 200 pounds in a barbell squat, she might decide that this is the most she would like to lift and then discontinue lifting because the goal has been reached. However, if the lifter then stops training, a week later she might discover that the most she can lift is 175 pounds. Muscle breaks down when not in use, as do lines of communication, skill mastery, and team cohesion in an IT department when the team stops training and improving.

Key Takeaway 8

The four types of work are business tasks, internal IT projects, changes, and unplanned recovery work that travels backward through the deployment pipeline.

Analysis

Business tasks are those that the IT department does for other departments so that they can better serve their customers. Internal IT projects improve the tools they use to complete business tasks. Changes are not specific to either of those categories, and usually involve updating or fixing a system. They are usually shorter tasks. Unplanned or recovery work takes time away from the first three types of work, and can be considered wasted time.

IT departments are not the only ones that can divide their work into these four categories. Any department that has a crisis and needs to interrupt its scheduled tasks to handle it performs unplanned work. For example, a human resources department has business tasks, which would be filling vacancies in other departments. It also has internal projects, which could be training to use HR software or attending team-building meetings. In HR, changes are regular, small tasks in either of those categories, such as making an edit to the employee onboarding slideshow or sending a copy of a job description to a supervisor to check whether it can be posted in a job opening.

Key Takeaway 9

The First Way of DevOps states that all work must flow from development to IT to the customer. This flow should be maximized and free of defects.

Analysis

The First Way of DevOps sounds like an ideal to which all types of work should aspire. If any system could guarantee that work will never be held up for flaws and that it will always be making progress toward distribution to the customer, it would be a very valuable system in all forms of manufacturing and programming. Companies that manage to decrease the rate of flaws naturally have an advantage over companies that tolerate a larger number of flaws. How a company goes about reducing the flow of flawed work may depend on its size and particular arrangement. An IT department with a large staff can devote many people to quality assurance, or assign code mentors to new programmers to check their work and teach them to be cleaner coders. A smaller company might only have enough people to complete normal IT tasks, so quality assurance would be part of their normal tasks to fit into the deployment pipeline, which is the flow of work from proposed to finished.

Key Takeaway 10

The Second Way of DevOps states that feedback should flow from the customer to IT, and from IT to development. It must be amplified to prevent problems, improve detection and recovery, and improve overall quality.

Analysis

One major challenge in the design of any product is that users require feedback to know whether their devices are working and how long they should wait before attempting the same operation again. For example, many websites change the color of links and buttons when the user clicks on them, registering that the website received that interaction and is working on delivering the new webpage. Keyboard keys depress, and keyboards on touch-screen devices react visually or with sounds, so that the user does not repeatedly press a button for no reason. Feedback in a deployment pipeline cuts out some of these repetitive behaviors that arise in similar situations. If a developer receives feedback that customers are satisfied with a product, the need to change it, add features, or patch minor bugs decreases. If, on the other hand, the feedback is negative, the importance of changing the product is relayed back to the developer, who raises the importance of perfecting the product.

Key Takeaway 11

The Third Way of DevOps states that a business's IT culture should support experimentation, risk-taking, and the learning and practice that facilitate mastery.

Analysis

Some of the most admired companies are known for taking big risks, some of which fail, and recovering quickly. Apple developed several unpopular devices, such as Apple TV, but its culture ensured that an unpopular device did not tie up resources, which the company quickly pivoted to another new and exciting project. Today Apple is better known for its successes than for its failures. Ideally, any business engaged in IT will encourage employees to experiment, fail fast, and then move on to the next best use of their resources if the risk did not pay off.

Key Takeaway 12

DevOps strategies apply to departments that already use other structures, use open source or proprietary software, or are of any size or flexibility.

Analysis

At various points, employees and executives at Parts Unlimited rejected the DevOps strategies because they were unfamiliar or ran against conventional wisdom. When they saw the advantages of a system like the kanban-style scheduling board or the complete documentation of changes, they generally changed their minds because the individuals became involved in its success.

Older organizations that added IT departments only when computers became useful in business, which could have been as recently as the 1980s, may have added the departments as experiments at first and may never have taken the step to fully integrate IT processes in other parts of the business. For example, HR is expected to be fully involved in every part of a business because it is responsible for filling vacancies anywhere they occur. IT might seem different because, for example, a restaurant chain might see IT as less important than the ability to source ingredients or pay workers. However, in parts of the world where computer systems are used to generate invoices, issue paychecks, and receive feedback from customers, IT is a core competency that is just as involved in every part of the company, and would benefit from the DevOps approach of bringing everyone into the IT super-tribe.

Author's Style

The Phoenix Project is a business allegory told as a novel with a first-person narrator, who happens to be an employee at a business where a DevOps transformation occurs. This narration style, styled after Goldratt's *The Goal*, guides the reader through the plot but does not deliver absolute guidelines or principles the way a typical DevOps book would. The lessons are delivered in the form of the narrator's personal revelations. Because he has many revelations throughout the book, some of which are good and some of which turn out to be misguided, the lessons to learn are unclear. The end of the book includes a guide that summarizes the principles and advantages of DevOps in a clearer format, but does not summarize all of the lessons that the main character learns.

The narrator has an assertive voice and delivers many judgments about his co-workers, some of which are harsh. He is not a paragon of responsible behavior, particularly in the moments when he is working with the chief information security officer and convinces him to abandon high standards for security and prevent auditors from observing a potentially extreme violation of customer data security. The narrator's outlook on some things, such as the motivations of certain employees and the worth of certain DevOps principles, changes over the course of the book.

There is a mix of specialized terminology throughout the book that may be difficult for some readers to understand even if they are well-versed in technology or development. The narrator is a former Marine and several other characters were in the military, so they often tell stories about their careers that include acronyms and refer to the paths that military careers generally take. The technological terms span a range of specializations, from development and virtualization to version control and security testing automation. Due to the use of the manufacturing model in the narrative, there is also specialized manufacturing terminology. Some terms that are highly technical, such as "cycle time," are never defined. Others that are coined for the principles of the book, such as how to "elevate" or "subordinate" a constraint, are also not fully defined.

Author's Perspective

The authors of *The Phoenix Project* have an extensive history in research for IT management and strategy, and have been involved in the growing popularity of the DevOps method in technology companies since DevOps was established in 2008. All three have worked in businesses that rely heavily on IT capabilities. In their summary of DevOps principles, they describe how these principles became part of their personal strategies, especially after witnessing the changes that these strategies made in the productivity of certain technology industry leaders. By using the novel style to tell the story of how DevOps principles change a specific business, they combine their own experiences as managers and developers into a realistic and informative allegory.

~~~~ END OF INSTAREAD ~~~~

Instaread on The Phoenix Project

Thank you for purchasing this Instaread book

Download the Instaread mobile app to get unlimited text & audio summaries of bestselling books.

Visit Instaread.co to learn more.

References

1. Ingram, David. "Corporate 'siloing' an obstacle to charging employees: prosecutor." *Reuters*. September 17, 2015. Accessed March 14, 2016. http://www.reuters.com/article/us-gm-settlement-individuals-idUSKCN0RH31B20150917

2. Rosen, Rebecca. "In Praise of Short-Term Thinking: For hundreds of years, economic observers have feared that machines were making human workers obsolete. In a sense, they've been right." *The Atlantic*. September 2015. Accessed March 25, 2016. http://www.theatlantic.com/business/archive/2015/09/jobs-automation-technological-unemployment-history/403576/

3. "Cycle Time." *Lean Manufacturing Glossary*. 2011. Accessed March 14, 2016. http://www.tpslean.com/glossary/cycledef.htm

CPSIA information can be obtained
at www.ICGtesting.com
Printed in the USA
LVOW04s0803140516
488253LV00029B/481/P